Playing Fair, Having Fun

A Kid's Guide to Sports and Games

Written by
Daniel Grippo

Illustrated by
R. W. Alley

ONE
CARING
PLACE

Abbey Press
St. Meinrad, IN 47577

For Mr. Al Hopkins, a wonderful coach and role model,
and for my childhood friends and teammates
and all the great games we played.

Text © 2004 Daniel Grippo
Illustrations © 2004 St. Meinrad Archabbey
Published by One Caring Place
Abbey Press
St. Meinrad, Indiana 47577

Library of Congress Catalog Number
2004104017

ISBN 978-0-87029-384-9

Printed in the United States of America

A Message to Parents, Teachers, and Other Caring Adults

Perhaps you remember, as I do, a simpler time, playing outside with friends after school, making things up as we went along. While it's true we played a lot of the same great games and sports that kids play today, it's also true that times have changed quite a bit in a generation.

Kids today face tremendous pressure when it comes to team sports. Schedules are demanding, expectations are high, and the competition can be fierce. The attention and fortunes lavished on professional athletes further distort the picture many kids (and adults) have about the place of sports in life and society.

Sometimes we adults only make matters worse. Some parents and coaches put excessive pressure on kids when it comes to sports. Others seem to live vicariously through the exploits of their child athletes. A few, unfortunately, set a poor example of sportsmanship at games.

In addition to all this, kids today are growing up with less parental supervision and a wide variety of computer and internet games that bring new creative possibilities but also new temptations and risks. It is, indeed, a brave new world of entertainment and recreation.

Now more than ever, kids need guidance when it comes to their recreational activities. This booklet is designed to help kids think about sports and games in new ways, so they can enjoy themselves while keeping things in perspective.

Play is the human creature's most spontaneous and joyous way of participating in God's creative—and recreative—activity. Sports and games help kids grow strong in mind and body. They also teach kids a lot about life—about sportsmanship, teamwork, cooperation, dealing with victory and setback, fairness, honesty, and personal responsibility.

All of us, adults as well as children, need to continually examine our attitudes about sports and games, to ensure that they remain healthy, renewing, and life-giving.

—Daniel Grippo

It's Great to Play!

Playing is fun, and it's good for you, too. When you play, you feel alive and happy. You run and jump and shout. You laugh and get excited.

You grow strong and healthy when you play. And you learn new things, too—about how to play different games and how to play well with others.

You can't play all the time, of course, because you have other things to do—like sleep and clean your room and go to school. But it's fine to play as long as you also do the things your parents and teachers ask you to do.

Enjoy God's Creation

God wants you to be happy. When you are laughing and having fun with others, God is happy too.

When you play, you get to be joyful and creative—like God. You can make up worlds in your mind, just as God created the world you live in.

Enjoy God's creation in all its wonder. It's time to play! Hurray!

You're Different—You're You!

Maybe Justin is bigger than you and always gets picked for teams first. Maybe Susie is fastest and always wins races. Some kids are good at sports, and other kids are good in different ways.

We all are special in some way. Be proud of who you are. The special things that you like to do are part of what make you YOU!

You may like to play on teams, or you may like to go hiking or ride your bike. There are lots of ways to play. You don't have to be the biggest or the fastest to have fun.

So Many Ways to Play

You don't need a lot of fancy toys or gear to have a good time. You can find things around the house to make up a whole play world!

You can play alone, with your best friend, or on a team. You can play with a puppy or kitten, with your brother or sister, or your mom or dad.

Think about all the things that are fun for you. Maybe you like to draw or sing or write stories. Make up your own games doing the things you like. Then teach them to your friends.

Play It Safe

Whether you're playing in your driveway or on a soccer field, you need to have the right safety gear—like a helmet or shin guards. Keep your gear in good shape and all in one place, so you know where to find it.

Every sport has safety rules to keep players from getting broken bones, or worse. Play by the rules, so no one gets hurt.

Have you ever watched "extreme sports" on TV? Those daring skiers and boarders look very cool. But TV doesn't often show the ones who crash and get hurt. Doing stunts like that is "extremely" risky. Leave it to the pros!

Worried About Messing Up?

Sometimes playing sports can make you nervous. Everyone is watching, and you don't want to mess up. You might think, "What if I drop the fly ball? What if I miss the goal? What if I come in last?"

We all mess up sometimes. Pro baseball players are good if they get a hit once every three times. That means they "mess up" two out of three times!

Some things in sports are very hard to do. But as you practice and try hard, you will see yourself getting better. Don't worry about messing up—just get in there and have a good time!

Coach Problems

Maybe your coach yells at you a lot, or doesn't let you play as much as you want. If you think your coach is being mean or unfair, try to talk to him or her. Ask what you can do to make things better. If things still don't work out, talk to your parents about what to do.

Sometimes your parent is your coach. If you feel your mom or dad is being too easy or too hard on you as a coach, talk with him or her at home after the game.

Parent Problems

Some parents get carried away watching you play sports. Maybe your dad yells at you from the sidelines, or your mom gets mad if you don't have a good game. This can make you feel bad, because you want your parents to be proud of you.

Let your parents know how you feel. When they understand they are making you feel bad, they can try to change.

Be sure to tell your parents thanks for all they do for you and your team. Thank your mom when she leaves work early to take you to practice. Thank your dad when he brings snacks and drinks for your team.

Play Fair

Sometimes kids you play against will play dirty or cheat. They might push you when the ref isn't watching or trip you when you're about to score a goal. They might say bad words or call you a bad name.

Just because other kids play dirty or cheat doesn't mean you have to. Believe in yourself. Play by the rules, even when no one is looking.

You'll always feel good about yourself, and that's the best feeling of all.

Be a Good Sport

It's lots more fun to win than to lose. But no one wins all the time.

If you win, it's fine to be happy, but don't brag about it or rub it in. Remember that it hurts to lose, so be nice to the other team.

If you lose, don't let it get you down. You don't need to blame the refs or your coaches or anybody—just try harder next time. Win or lose, be sure to say, "Good game" to the other team.

Being a good sport means hanging in there, no matter what. Remember, there's always another day and another game to play!

Time Out

There's more to life than sports. If sports take up all your time, you'll be too tired to do your schoolwork or spend time with your family and friends.

Everyone needs a vacation sometimes. It's okay to take time out during the year just to relax, without being on a team. It's nice to give your family a break, too, because being on a team means lots of planning and driving for your family.

If you like playing on teams all year round, and it's okay with your family, that's fine, too. The most important thing is for sports to be fun for you and your family.

Video Games

Video games and internet games can be a lot of fun. You can battle aliens in a faraway galaxy or create a perfect city. Sometimes it's hard to stop playing.

Do you play when you should be doing other things, like homework? Do you spend a lot of your time alone playing video games? Do your wrists or hands or eyes hurt after you play? If you answered "yes" to any of these questions, you could be spending too much time playing.

If you only play video games once in a while, just for a little while each time, you'll feel better and enjoy the games more.

Board Games

Playing board games with friends or family is a good time. It helps if you keep smiling and have fun even when things aren't going your way.

Sure, you might lose some "money" or "hotels" or "armies," but that doesn't mean you've lost anything really important.

Many board games depend on luck, so there's no way to control what happens. You may have good or bad luck, but you can always have fun if you remember that it's just a game.

Sports, Games, and Life

You can learn a lot about life from playing sports and games. You learn that, win or lose, you can still have a good time. What counts the most is having fun and enjoying the people you play with.

You learn that playing fair is more important than always winning. You learn to make time for all the good things in your life—sports, family, friends, school, and time alone, too.

When you think about it, you really learn a lot when you play. And you get to have so much fun while you're at it. That's why playing is such a great thing!

Daniel Grippo is the editor of CareNotes, a division of Abbey Press publications. He is the author of several Abbey Press books, including *Loneliness Therapy* and *Healing Thoughts for Hurting Hearts* (August 2004). His wish for the world: that adults would work less, play more, share their toys, and learn how to get along.

R. W. Alley is the illustrator for the popular Abbey Press adult series of Elf-help books, as well as an illustrator and writer of children's books. He lives in Barrington, Rhode Island, with his wife, daughter, and son. See a wide variety of his works at: www.rwalley.com.